INDUSTRIAL DONCASTER
IN PICTURES

Industrial Doncaster
IN PICTURES

PAUL WALTERS & GILES BREARLEY

WHARNCLIFFE PUBLISHING

First Published in 1998 by
Wharncliffe Publishing
an imprint of
Pen and Sword Books Limited,
47 Church Street, Barnsley,
South Yorkshire. S70 2AS

For up-to-date information on other titles produced under the
Wharncliffe imprint, please telephone or write to:

> **Wharncliffe Publishing**
> **FREEPOST**
> **47 Church Street**
> **Barnsley**
> **South Yorkshire S70 2BR**
> **Telephone (24 hours): 01226 - 734555**

ISBN: 1-871647-50-9

Cover photograph:
The Hatfield Moor Well Head blowout 1981

Printed in Great Britain by
St. Edmundsbury Press, Bury St. Edmunds, Suffolk.

Cover Design by Paul Wilkinson

INTRODUCTION

Michael Walters. Photographer. 1933 to 1994.

MICHAEL WALTERS was born in 1933 and raised at his parents home in Mexborough, in the industrial heartland of South Yorkshire. Mike was the son of a commercial photographer, who during World War 2 had worked for the Daily Mirror newspaper.

Mike was educated at Mexborough Grammar School and Worksop College. He served with the Royal Army Ordnance Corps, rising to the rank of captain. On leaving the Army in 1955, he set up his own photographic company, recording for posterity a great many of the major industrial projects which shaped the area and its' people. His reputation developed and over the years, M.T. Walters and Associates grew into one of Europes most prestigious photographic companies, with assignments in such far flung places as Malawi, Trinidad and Tobago, Jamaica, Canada and the United States, in addition to numerous European countries.

During the 1980's, Mike was considered to be one of the leading British industrial photographers and this led to varied and sometimes dangerous subjects to photograph. In December 1981, a small exploratory oil drilling well near Doncaster, hit a large pocket of natural gas which on reaching the surface, exploded with disastrous consequences.

The one time right hand man of the famous oilwell firefighter 'Red' Adaire, 'Boots' Hanson, was flown in to deal with the ensuing blaze and cap the well. MT Walters & Associates were called in by the owner of the well to record the incident on film and a small selection of the photographs taken during the incident appear in this volume. Many of these photographs were taken by Mikes' own right hand man

Roy Wooding, who worked with him for many years.

Of course, Mike did not confine his work to exploding oil wells. With clients as diverse as Danish Bacon and the National Coal Board, his work covered a wide spectrum and in 1986, he was awarded the National Architectural Award by the British Institute of Professional Photographers for his photograph of the Reform Club in London's Pall Mall.

During his career, Michael amassed a collection of some 240,000 negatives of his work. Each one numbered and dated, with basic information attached to it, which has become the Michael Walters Industrial Archive.

His own interests were centred around the history of the Industrial Revolution and Ecclesiastical Architecture, which he recorded on his travels and which he intended to make into a book when he retired from professional life. Unfortunately, he was never to achieve this as his health deteriorated and sadly, he died in October 1994 at the age of 61.

Michael left a wife Pat, who he married in 1960 and two sons. Gareth, who at the time of publication lives and works in Hong Kong as an art director and Paul who like his father, has his own photographic company producing pictures for the international media market.

Paul Walters. 1998.

THE MICHAEL WALTERS INDUSTRIAL ARCHIVE

The photographs featured in this book are available as 10″x 8″ prints mounted in a high quality frame, at a cost of £18.00 each including postage and packaging. To place your order, please write with cheque payable to:

Worldwide Photography Ltd.

at: The Studios, Dolcliffe Road, Mexborough. South Yorkshire S64 9AZ
Telephone: (01709) 582474

HATFIELD MOOR NATURAL GAS DRILLING EXPLOSION.

On Monday December 20th 1981, an oil drilling team was working on Hatfield Moor. At a depth of 100 feet, the drill pierced the roof of a massive pocket of natural gas. The gas immediately shot up the borehole under considerable pressure.

On reaching the surface it mixed with the air and hot exhaust fumes from a nearby generator. The ensuing explosion and fire severely damaged the drilling rig, various portable buildings and a large proportion of the wellhead equipment which was nearby. It was sheer good fortune that no one was seriously injured or killed in the blast.

The scene of the accident was attended by fire crews drawn from the surrounding three counties, but they lacked the training or experience to deal with such an incident. The natural gas explosion at Hatfield Moor was the first such event ever to have occurred in Britain.

Some fifty firemen were on the scene, but they were at a loss as to what was the correct action to take. They felt that endlessly pumping water onto the fire was a pointless exercise and it was decided to let the gas simply burn itself out. Unfortunately, strong and variable winds spread the flames and the general area around the wellhead also began to catch fire.

At 12-20pm the steel drilling rig collapsed onto the main equipment compound crushing several portable buildings. The drilling crew frantically tried to move the remaining equipment and portable offices away from the area around the fire, but a great deal of equipment was crushed or burned. As the fire was still blazing on Tuesday 22nd of December, it was considered that expert advice was needed to tackle the problem and it was decided to request the Texas oilwell trouble shooter 'Boots' Hanson, to tackle the blaze. Meanwhile the fire services were having to keep a 24 hour watch on the site and the Assistant Divisional Officer for Doncaster Fire Service, Mr Gordon Fawcett, was forced to admit, 'The fire is beyond our capabilities'.

Following the acceptance of the job by 'Boots' Hanson and his team, an aircraft hangar at Royal Air Force Lindholme was made available for the assembly of plant and equipment, in readiness for the arrival of 'Boots' and his team.

At the time, 'Boots' Hanson was 55 years of age and following 23 years working with 'Red' Adaire, he had formed his own company in partnership with his colleague of many years, 'Coots' Matthews. Inevitably, the company was called 'Boots and Coots!' 1982 was a very busy year for 'Boots & Coots', with 52 blowouts and fires dealt with worldwide, up to the point where they received the call asking them to come to Hatfield Moor.

They arrived on a scheduled flight on the Wednesday and were promptly airlifted to Royal Air Force Lindholm. Boots' first request on arrival at Lindholm was that he be flown round the site to enable him to carry out an aerial survey. Following this and a visit to the site on the ground, he organised an increase in the supply of water directed at the blaze. To facilitate this, hoses were laid from the mains which passed alongside the adjacent main road and booster pumps were linked to these hoses to increase the pressure at the fire. While this was going on, the weather had deteriorated and snow was now covering the ground.

Once he had fully assesed the situation, 'Boots' Hanson gave a press conference where he detailed his plans for fighting the blaze.

He envisaged it would take four days. First of all it would be necessary to clear the site of debris and damaged equipment. Following this operation he would decide whether the flames were to be extinguished with water or by an explosion. While all this was going on, his right hand man Clayton Berry, would liaise closely with the Fire Brigade crews, advising them as to the needs of the team and how they were to work together. It was commented that Mr Hanson and Mr Berry would be missing yet another Christmas at home, something which was becoming a regular feature of their lives at that time.

'Boots' also observed that this was his first job in Europe since 1977, when he was called in to plug a blowout on the North Sea rig, Ekofisk Bravo. The press were also keenly interested in what 'Boots & Coots' would be paid for the Hatfield Moor job. 'Boots's only reply was, 'A damn site less than if you'd used Red Adaire'.

By this time, scores of Television, radio and press reporters and their backup teams were on site and satellite television carried live coverage of the drama to a worldwide audience.

Heat screens were now erected and placed near the wellhead to protect the firemen who were directing the hoses onto the seat of the fire.

Boots' plan for capping the well was to fit a new wellhead, blow off valve and pipe assembly to the head of the well, diverting the flames up the pipe and away from the point where his team were working. Boots was then able to operate a snuffing device to kill off the flames. The operation was carried out sucessfully and cheers were heard from the onlookers as Boots and his team suceeded in bolting the new wellhead into place. Once he had the well under control, Boots allowed the gas to escape in a controlled manner. It was then once more set alight, as it was considered safer to burn off the gas than let it escape into the atmosphere unburned. The final part of the operation was to pump mud and water down the borehole where it compressed and formed a plug cutting off the gas supply to the surface.

s dusk descends over the snow clad round, the blazing well could be seen for iiles around. *44189a. 23/12/81*

A fireman continues the struggle to contain the blaze. *44189b. 23/12/81*

he wreckage of the drilling rig, following ie explosion. *44190. 24/12/81*

The fire spread rapidly and swiftly engulfed nearby offices and storage areas. *44192. 24/12/81.*

Royal Air Force Lindholme made available an aircraft hangar, enabling the team to assemble their equipment under cover. *44196. 24/12/81*

Temporary pipes had to be laid to meet the huge demand for water by the firefighters. *44197. 26/12/81*

Teams worked around the clock in freezing conditions, to lay waste pipes to draw off excess water which was collecting around the wellhead and hampering operations. *44198. 26/12/81*

Film and Television crews record the event as they unfold. *44201. 26/12/81*

iremen look on in despair. This certainly
as a new situation to them.
4204. 30/12/81

Boots Hanson and Clayton Berry carry
out an inspection near the wellhead.
44205. 30/12/81

like Walters' fellow photograpgher Roy
Vooding, is caught waiting to take another
ction shot as the drama unfolds.
4207. 5/1/82.

In order that the firemen could get as
close to the wellhead as possible, heat
shields were set up and water sprayed at
the flames. *44208. 5/1/82*

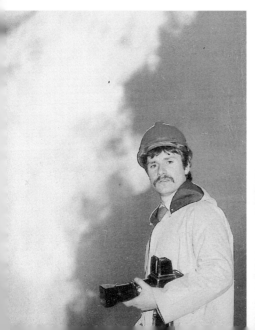

Boots and Clayton discuss strategy.
44220. 6/1/82.

The new large wellhead pipe is assembled
ready for positioning over the wellhead.
44221. 6/1/82

Chatting with fire crew, Boots ensures all
crew members are carefully briefed on
their part in the operation. *44222. 6/1/82.*

Carrying out a final reconnisance before
the action starts. *44223. 6/1/82*

final check on the valve which was to be
owered over the wellhead. *44226. 6/1/82*

The valve and wellhead pipe are lifted by
crane to get them into position.
44225. 6/1/82.

he firemen have the water jets full on while
he valve is moved to the wellside. *44229.
/1/82.*

Following an operation of great
precision, the valve and pipe are now in
position and one of Boots' crew ascends
a ladder to help free the crane arm which
has locked onto the pipe. *44230. 6/1/82.*

Danger over. The blaze is now controlled by the new valve. In order to fit the valve, it was necessary to install side pipes to reduce the pressure at the wellhead, while it was being fitted. 44216/44236. 6/1/82.

The fire crews stand watching as Boots team operate the valve.

Boots Hanson and Clayton Berry enjoy lighter moment now that the job is done. *44233. 6/1/82.*

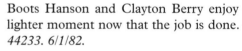

Two views of the winter meeting at Doncaster Racecourse in 1978 are captured here. The photograph was commissioned by Peglar Hattersley. Brassfounders of Doncaster, to promote the new VIP Suite. *C40506. 27/2/78.*

Staff and customers in action at Frasers Butchers Shop, Waterdale. All parties concerne
seem to be enjoying the business in hand. *9379. 1/7/65.*

The new
Rockware Glass
factory soon after
its' opening.
32898. 7/12/72.

Commissioned by Danish Bacon to demonstrate the versatility of their delivery fleet. This shot is part of a set showing the DBC fleet in well known locations such as this one at Doncaster race course. The ice cream van on the right belongs to Massarellas, who still trade from their Doncaster depot. *17489. 1/7/68.*

The accompanying photographs show some of the first passengers awaiting the arrival of their bus, at the new North Bus Station, while the early risers get their vehicles into the multi storey car park first. /14009/14003. 4/10/67.

This photograph was commissioned by Mowlems to show the early stages of their construction of the North Bus Station. *10500. 4/9/66.*

The Worshipful the Mayor, Alderman Mrs Stenson officially opens the recently completed North Bus Station and Multi Storey Car Park. *14205 4/10/67.*

A fine shot of the Winning Post pub with its' most appropriate sign. Sadly the sign, a fine example of pub sign art, no longer stands. *6560. 16/10/62.*

The Parts Department of Kennings Motor Company soon after it was equipped with a new and up to date racking system for spares. *12079. 20/4/67.*

Taken for the East Midland Gas Board, this photograph shows the comprehensive display of gas appliances, to tempt customers away from coal, the dominant fuel of the day, with the cleanliness and convenience of gas. *5096. 29/6/61.*

Two of the staff at British Ropes check the quality and dimensions of finished rope during the latter stages of manufacture. The rope being checked is a thirteen and a half inch circumference rope. British Ropes was a premier supplier of ropes to a worldwide clientel. The company was formed in 1924, with the amalgamation of the British Wire and the Fibre Rope and Binder Twine manufacturing companies. The oldest company in the group was the partnership of T Dyson & William Smith, which was formed in 1782. *18383. 23/7/68.*

A group of Danish businessmen being conducted around British Ropes during a tour of inspection, demonstrating the high standards applied in this industry. *14092. 4/3/68.*

A fine shot of wire ropes being wound onto reels at British Ropes. *4115. 29/3/60.*

Bottles being produced at Rockware Glass. *C32882. 29/11/72.*

This photograph shows the new batch house nearing completion at Rockware Glass. This structure is used to house raw materials used in glass making. *14380. 4/10/67.*

Tractors at the final stages of assembly in the International Harvester plant. Tractors from this factory were exported all over the world and the company was a true sucess story for Doncaster. The equipment produced by the Doncaster plant was: The Deering and McCormic range of tractors, with harvesters, reapers, mowers, rakes, tillers, binders and turbines. *10288. 23/6/66*

The final assembly and testing shop at International Harvesters. *10287. 23/6/66.*

During the 60's and 70's, Michael undertook a great deal of work for the Stanley tool company. In addition to covering their range of world renowned carpentry tools, this shot of the Ladies versus Men soccer match in Doncaster shows the lighter side of factory life, with an early 70's example of cross dressing by the male employees. 31781. 27/4/71.

Four star meeting of the Danish Bacon sales team at the Earl of Doncaster Hotel. The Danish Bacon company has been trading in the United Kingdom since 1902. *8113. 11/5/64.*

A fine photograph of Markham Main Colliery from the south west showing the upcast ascent gear. *1516. 2/5/56.*

The scene on the surface of Markham Main Colliery in 1951. The winding gear can be seen in the background to the right of the smokestack *5285. 29/8/51*

Internal photograph of the refurbished chemists shop. This photograph was comissioned by the Bakelite Company. *5529. 21/11/61.*

Another photograph comissioned by the Bakelite Company following refurbishment of the ladies hair salon. *5533. 21/11/64.*

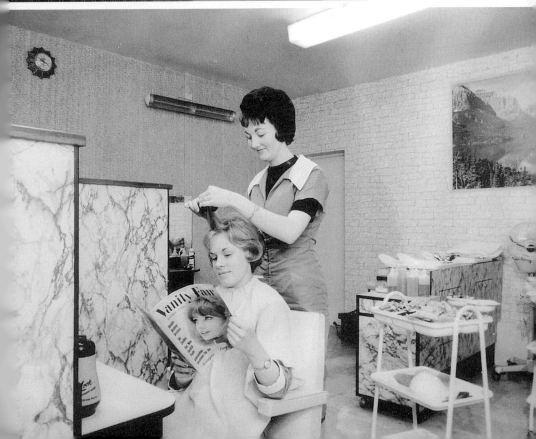

Two photographs taken for Wimpey Construction, of the Mill Lane site at Armthorpe above being on the day they moved onto the site. *11933 & 11934. 4/4/67.*

A superbly detailed photograph of the Coalite chemical plant which utilised the by products of coal for commercial purposes. The plant produced Coalite smokeless fuel and numerous chemicals for use in other industries. *32180. 28/6/72.*

A fine view of the pithead winding gear of Rossington Colliery which operated the skip shaft equipment. *8692. 3/12/64.*

The main fan drift of Rossington Colliery photographed from the north. *10517. 16/9/66*

Norwest Construction team at work on the installation of the new head gear in the autumn of 1963. *7274. 5/10/63.*

Rossington Colliery in 1968. Work is seen here on the new fan drift. This project was a major investment for the colliery at that time. *18062 & 18066. 27/11/68.*

The original owners of the colliery were the Rossington Main Colliery Company Limited, which was incorporated in 1911 by Lord Aberconway and Sir C.E. Ellis HCB GBE. Throughout its' life, this colliery regularly achieved output of the order of 750,000 tons per annum.

The thickener is here under construction at the new Coal Preparation Plant of Bentley
Colliery. The thickener was the device which seperated the coal dust from the water used
in the washing process. A thickening agent was added to the water to speed up separation
of the fine coal dust from the washing water before it was returned to the general system
or re-used for washing. This colliery had been the scene of a major pit disaster in 1932
when 45 men were killed. *5433. 29/8/61.*

The opening night of the Groves Club at Conisborough with the staff in readiness for the initial onslaught. The Opening Team from left to right. Peggy Fitz. June Wesley, Pat Taylor Stewardess) Marilyn Granville, Sheila Foweather, May Needham and Ron Taylor Steward). *C40551/1. 16/3/78.*

The first committee of the Groves club pictured at the opening. The Mayor of Doncaster and the Brewery representatives also attended. *Standing:* Johnny Young, Eric Squires, ohn Duffy, Billy Smith, Willis Gomersall, Pat Downing, Billy McArthur, Eddie Bond, Mayor of Doncaster, Albert Carmody, Mr Robinson Director Camerons Brewery. *Seated:* Vic Goddard, Jimmy Rose, Robert Bond, Billy Wright, Tommy Woodhead. *C40551/2*

The recently completed Coal Preparation Plant at Cadeby colliery. *3493. 2/5/59.*

Interior photograph of the refurbished Winding House at Cadeby Colliery. *1353. 13/1/5(*

An exterior photograph of the improvements in progress on the shaft and winding house at Cadeby colliery. *1352. 13/1/56.*

The heap stead under repair by Norwest Construction. In the background can be seen the chimney of the steam winder of Cadeby Colliery. The area plans of the National Coal Board for the 1970's anoted that Cadeby had the most extensive workable reserves in the area. This fact made the rapid closure of this colliery even more surprising when it happened. *1240 20/10/55.*

Norwest Construction undertaking improvements to the surface installations at Cadeby colliery. *1180. 6/9/55.*

The extensive refurbishment of Cadeby colliery fan drift. This was part of the modernisation programme undertaken in the late 1950's. Other work included new heap teads and the construction of a new coal preparation plant to modern standards. The original shafts at Cadeby were sunk in 1889. *1987. 10/1/57.*

This photograph was taken at the Steetley Limestone Quarry late in 1955. At this time and for many years previously, this had been the largest limestone quarry in South Yorkshire. When the author was a boy and living in Mexborough, he and his friends were always fascinated by the rumbling explosions from the quarry as ever more of the face was blasted away. *1216. 7/10/55.*

A photograph commissioned by the Nestlé Company, to demonstrate the high standard of window displays. This display was at Farmers Grocery shop, which was situated on the main road in Denaby. It is interesting to observe that the total prize money available in the Nestlé national window display competition was only £5,000. *3336. 20/2/59.*

The Foxwell under construction. This was to be Mike Walters' home and was situated at the end of Old Denaby village in a wooded and quarried landscape. Previously a cottage had stood on this site but it was demolished to make way for the new house. The quarry workings which surrounded the site of the house ceased operations in the early 1900's. The house remained the Walters' family home until 1995 when, following Mike's death, the property was sold.

The team from William Press & Sons Limited unload pipes on the CEGB ground at Denaby Lane in preparation for the new drainage project. In the background can be seen the power station. The William Press Ltd works were situated just across the road from the power station, so transport was not a major problem !
432. 23/10/67.

A presentation by Imperial Chemical Industries Ltd. (ICI) for services rendered, to D
Lowe. The presentation took place at the ICI Powder Works, which had operated on th
same site at Old Denaby for over 100 years. The plant closed shortly after this event.
6562. 28/9/62.

The new Bartol Plastics Limited factory at Edlington. The placing of the new factory at Edlington was the result of local initiatives. Previously situated at Swinton, the move to newer and substantially larger premises followed a period of rapid expansion which the old Swinton factory could not accomodate. *32897. December 1972.*

A long service award being presented on behalf of the Steetley Group by Mr W tocks. This presentation was made at the White Greyhound ub. Sadly, the recipient annot be traced. Steetley ave actively quarried in the rea for many years. *9987. 1/2/66.*

This photograph taken for Milne Scaffolding who had been hired by Royal Air Force Finningley, to erect a temporary VIP stand for its' famous Battle of Britain open day. An event not to be missed. In the photograph can be seen late model Vulcan bombers on their hardstandings while a fighter aircraft trails smoke during his fly past. *32553. 16/9/72*

One of Denniff's lorries being loaded at the Finningley sand and gravel plant, which was an integral part of the village economy for many years. A similar quarry operated by the same company at Rossington, regularly produced over 1,000 tonnes per day. *10770. 23/7/61.*

The newly erected head gear of Brodsworth overshadows the older buildings of the colliery. This mine was originally sunk by the Battie Wrightsons of Cusworth Hall. The Brodsworth Main Colliery Company Limited was originally formed on September 7th 1905. The company spent a, staggering for the time, sum of £1,350,000 before any coal was produced from this mine. *4889. 20/4/61.*

A photograph taken at Norton House, Sprotborough, formerly the home of Mike Walters' father. The house was later sold to Sir Graham Kirkham, having originally been built for a former director of Bartol Plastics. The gardener seems deeply concerned by the sight of the model posing with the Stanley electric garden shears. *9130. 27/4/65.*

A promotional photograph of the latest Vulcan boiler. In the 1960's it was fashionable to place items in unusual surroundings, making this shot in the height of fashion for the day The photograph features model Launa McDonahue, whom Michael employed frequently and at the time of writing heads Manchesters Pamela Holt model agency. 190. 18/5/65.

Little has changed in Tickhill since this photograph was taken. The village has man
points of interest, with some buildings traceable back to Norman times. To the left of th
pond can be seen part of the castle wall, which was severely damaged during the Civ
War, though much of the moat, garden and curtain wall remain. *1871. 10/11/61.*

Photograph taken for Bierrum & Partners showing construction under way at Thorpe Marsh Power Station. The Bond Mini Car in the foreground, pre dates the escapades of Del Boy and his Reliant Robin twenty years later. *5310. 7/9/61.*

A fine photograph of Ferrybridge Power Station undergoing rebuilding and modernisation. The modernisation was essential to reduce the level of acid rain, which results from using coal in the generating process. This could be carried as far afield as Norway. *10727. 14/11/66.*

The newly completed reconstruction of Ferrybridge Power Station. This photograph has to be taken very early in the morning to avoid traffic on the A1 which crosses the shot in the foreground. *14069. 3/10/67.*

An exterior photograph of the newly completed mill taken for Bierrum & Sons Ltd., builders of the mill. The mill was located alongside the river Trent. Excellently sited amidst agricultural land, this mill was where Spillers produced their animal feeds. The Spillers company started life in London in 1887 and enjoyed continuous expansion to the point where it became the leading millers in the United Kingdom. Mike Walters visited the mill on numerous occasions during its' construction and after, when Spillers wished to update their brochures. The selection of shots which follows gives a good impression of what mill life was like at that time. *9581. 13/8/65.*

The loaded bags, having been stitched closed are loaded onto pallettes prior to despatch. *4701. 14/12/60.*

Bags being filled at the Spillers animal feed mill in Gainsborough. *6555. 16/10/62.*

Demand and output was very high. Here stock awaits despatch. *4703. 14/12/60*

The staff canteen buzzes with conversation during a welcome break. *4175. 14/12/60.*

The weigh bridge office staff hard at it. Note, not a computer in sight, even the typewriter is manual. The large Avery scales dial at the rear gives a weight for lorries full and empty as they bring in raw materials and take away finished product.
4698. 14/12/60.

The laboratory and testing centre where the high standards are set and quality constantly monitored. *4699. 14/12/60.*

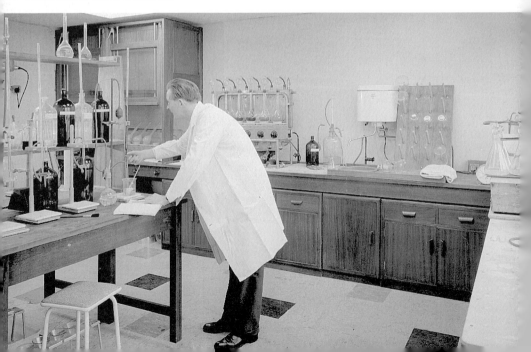

Reminiscent of 'The Hello Girls'. The equipment may have changed but the message stays the same. 'Putting you through now'!
4697. 14/12/60.

Madame Florence, the prominent ladies outfitters. Shown here at the relocated address, which is where the new Job Centre was built in Montague Square. The shop was previously situated in Bank Street. *6896. 4/4/63.*

This shot of High Street in Mexborough, taken in 1964 whilst traffic was still allowed free access, shows a range of well known names. Of the business' featured, only Lords opticians still trade in Mexborough. *1410. 18/3/64.*

Two photographs taken for East Midlands Gas Board showing a promotion in Claytons on High Street, Mexborough. *2084/5. 5/3/57.*

Hot Metal! Typesetting in the early days. These Linotype machines produced lines of type or 'slugs' which were arranged into pages and 'locked up' in a 'chase' (metal frame), as shown in the photograph on the left. Note the size of the room needed to house these machines, as compared to todays 'desktop' computer typesetting.

From right to left: George Shaw, Dick Ridyard (sub editor) and Len Sockett caught by the camera composing pages for the latest edition of the South Yorkshire Times. Wooden or metal blocks, 'furniture' as it was called, wedged the type against the 'chase'. This could then be lifted and taken to the printing machine.

The girls working in the binding room of the South Yorkshire Times. At the time these shots were taken, the binding room was situated on the upper floor of the High Street premises. Among those who may well be recognised by some are Edith Walker and Jessie Johnson. *3744/3745. 3/9/59.*

In 1964, Heinz launched a nationwide roadshow to introduce the British public to the preparations already on sale in the United States. This photograph was commissioned by Heinz and shows the band in full swing at the Empress Ballroom. Wonder what they had for supper after the show? *3925A. 18/2/64.*

Professional model Sue Gresham is here seen having the final touches put to her appearance immediately prior to the next shot. Also 'in shot' for once is Mike Walters, on the left and to the right of the photograph are Fred Ridout and Brian Wadsworth of Redfyres. The photographs taken in this set formed the basis of a national advertising campaign by Redfyres. *B66666. July 1969.*

This photograph was commissioned by the Barnsley British Co-Operative Society to promote their door to door delivery service. The shot was used as a reminder to customers, not to forget to cancel their milk deliveries when going on holiday. The house featured in the photograph is situated on Doncaster Road. Irene Darwyn models together with her daughter Ann and Mike's son, Gareth. The milkman is played by Jeff Wademan. *3926A. 4/12/59.*

Generations of South Yorkshire's grooms descended upon Alexandre's for their made to measure wedding and 'going away' suits. It is the author's belief that at least some of the tailors who were employed by Alexandre's, suffered from St Vitus Dance. A view based upon his own experiences! *7052. 12/8/63.*

Carlines were one of the first to set up in Mexborough using the supermarket approach to shopping. They eventually had a number of branches in the towns around South Yorkshire. This shot is of their Mexborough store which was across from the Montagu Arms. 14169. 4/10/67.

he Ferryboat Inn has a very long history in Mexborough, some believe it goes back to
e 1500's. Doug and Vi Watson took over the licence in the early 1960's and made the
b into a very popular place for many years.
his shot of the bottom bar shows their fine collection of miners lamps, which at the time
ere the talk of the area. *894. 11/11/56.*

riginal oak beams give a traditional character to the Ferryboat Inn. This photograph of
e top bar reveals that few things, except the landlord's name and the prices, have
anged. *1895. 11/11/56.*

Mexborough Grammar School football team excelled itself by winning the Engli
Schoolboys championship for the second time in 1974. On this photograph can be se
the winning team, their trainers and coach.

Looking from the upper floor window we can see resident Art teacher Mike Disl
relaxing with a cigarette. This clearly demonstrates that the no smoking rule exclud
the staff. *C37250. 23/1/75.*

Yorkshire Schools Individual Champions
English Schools Individual Semi Finalists 1974-1975

Back Row:
D Carns, J Edwards, R Bennett, J Hurt, G Rowe, R Fernley, I Whitlam, R Roberts,
Telling, M Stanley, G Roberts, At right hand end Mr G.W. Shield, Mr A. Scotter.
Front Row:
J Schofield, R Cooper, J Wrights, F Wild, M Sanna, P Hatfield, D Smith. (Absent fro
shot is R Tyler)

red Ward traded as a greengrocer in Mexborough for many years, selling fruit and
getables from a stall in the Market and a shop in the High Street. He also had a
holesale depot on Pym Road, from which he supplied other retailers in the area. The
uthor has fond childhood memories of Fred, donning his long black overcoat and trilby
at, while overseeing his army of teenage school leavers as they loaded and unloaded
rries or unpacked wooden boxes of fruit.
lso visible in the upper right of this shot is what remained of the Montague Hospital.
t the time this photograph was taken, what remained of the Hospital buildings were
eing used as a surgery by Dr Porter. *0274. 14/6/66.*

incent Matthews is seen here
rving one of his prepared
eals, which he hoped would
crease the business done by
s High Street café.
7519. 25/5/64.

Mexborough Urban District Council held an annual competition for the best kep council house garden. The winner in 1959 had obviously put in a great deal of effort or this Cowper Road garden. *3720. 18/8/59.*

'You'll always get fixed up at Leslie Haigh's', was good advice passed down to the autho from his father. Leslie Haigh the gents outfitters traded in the town for over 25 years. Thi property in Post Office Square is currently occupied by Ideal Travel. W & A Carpet which can be seen to the left of Haigh's in this shot, closed shortly after it was taken an the premises were then used by Tom Athron trading as Shentons Estate Agency. Tom late retired and sold the business to the W.H. Brown Estate Agency Group who still trad from these premises. *44243. November 1979.*

This photograph was commissioned by the manager of Mexborough Power Station to support a request for the resurfacing of the internal roadways. As a coal fired power station, its' internal road system was in regular use by heavy vehicles. *3255. 19/12/58.*

Mike Walters' studios at Dolcliffe Road underwent substantial alterations in order to effect a complete conversion from a chapel to a fully equipped photographic studio. *0154. 14/4/66.*

John Clayton appears in this shot taken for Nestlé in his shop in Mexborough.
3421. 26/11/59.

Alan Bracked, Leslie Taylor and Carol Ford discuss the requirements for the next shot on a set for Red Fyres in Mike's Studio at Dolcliffe Road. For commercial photography plenty of floor space was needed.
7714. 31/3/64.

The roundabout which forms the junction of Doncaster Road and the Relief Road.

The roof of the National School can be seen in the background behind the Electricity Showrooms.

Following the closure of the Electricity Showrooms, the premises were used as a gymnasium for a while, but are currently occupied by Adam Window Centre and Posies Florists. *25083. 20/5/70.*

The Montague Arcade was built at the turn of the century on the site of an old quarry. To the left of the photograph can be seen Hadwins the Outfitters. Each August used to see a parade of anxious schoolboys waiting to be fitted for their green Grammar School blazers in readiness for their elevation into the big time!

None of the businesses shown in this photograph remain today other than Claytons, on the far left which relocated to a nearby site not long afterwards. *6686. 4/11/62.*

The annual Mexborough Trades Fair was held at the Barnsley British Co-Operative Society's Bakery premises just off Church Street, Mexborough. These premises are currently used by the Coltran Wire Products Company. *14396. 27/10/67.*

Mexborough St John The Baptist Church Choir 1975.
Back row left to right.
Laurence Spratt (Curate), Andrew Squires, Steven Brooks, Ian Hanby, Ian Campbell, Gareth Walters, Richard Welland, Mark Henson.
Third Row left to right.
Neil Davis, Darren Eccles, David Wassell, Martin Waddington, Michael Campbell, John Stuart,(Choir master 1966 to 1985), Harry Hazeldean, David Staples (Vicar).
Second Row left to right.
Paul Irland, John Hazeldean, Nicholas Heald, Ian Ravenscroft, Nigel Tordoff, Nigel Ravenscroft, Unknown, Richard Adley, Mark Vicars.
First Row left to right.
Jonathan Bailey, Unknown, Christopher Salt, Unknown, Andrew McLauchlin, Unknown, Richard Tordoff, Paul Wilson.

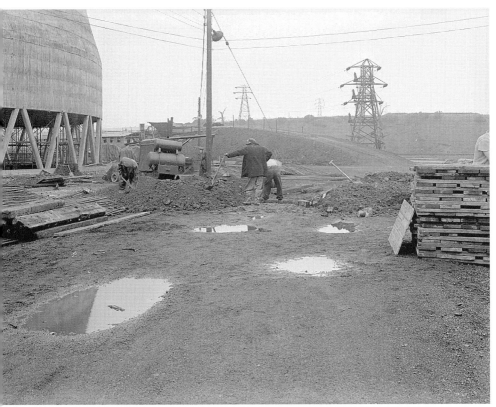

his photograph comissioned by Mitchell Construction Ltd., of Mexborough Power
ation having the finishing touches put to it. It looks as though it's been another cold
et June! *1599. 12/6/56.*

he roundabout on the Relief Road adjacent to the current location of the bus station.
096. 20/5/70.

STUDIO AND PRODUCT PHOTOGRAPHS.

Mike's studios at the corner of Hampden Road and Dolcliffe Road in Mexborough were used extensively for interior settings for much of his commercial work. The following photographs are extremely interesting as they show not only the products of the time, but the fashions in advertising.

Taken for Bachelors, a photograph of Quick Dried Carrott Strips. Not a product which seems to have caught on ! *0567. 22/9/66.*

Commissioned by the Danish Bacon Company, this photograph shows 'Schonhuts Succulent Super Sausages', almost disappointingly produced at their Rawmarsh factory. This brand was added to the Danish Bacon range. 2259. 13/6/57.

Mike at work in the 'office'. At the time, this was one of the most advanced photographic studios in the country, with its design inspired by the pioneering Scandinavian studios of the 1960's. The client in this case was the Doncaster advertising agency, Colbears. *114351. 24/10/67.*

The Hamax range of cleaners and disinfectants was produced in Mexborough and their delivery vans were well known throughout the region for many years. *2513. 1/2/58.*

An unknown model shows the latest range of Truline underwear. *7260. 30/9/63.*

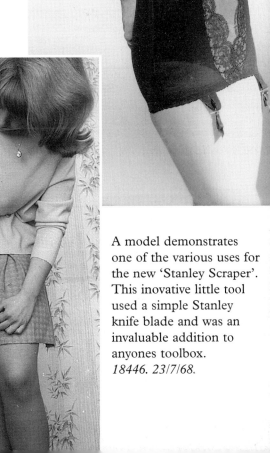

A model demonstrates one of the various uses for the new 'Stanley Scraper'. This inovative little tool used a simple Stanley knife blade and was an invaluable addition to anyones toolbox. *18446. 23/7/68.*

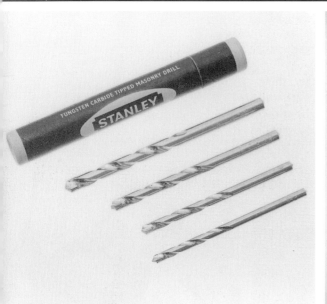

A promotional photograph for Stanley tools. This shot was to show the customers that Tungsten Carbide was now being used to tip their masonry bits. Tungsten Carbide, common on such drills today, was a buzz term to use to prospective customers in the early seventies. *29599. 22/6/72.*

George Milsom held a managerial position at the South Yorkshire Times and is seen here in this double exposure shot entitled 'Reflections in Profit'. Although still used, this effect is now much simpler to achieve in the computer rather than the camera. *8836B. 14/1/65.*

Photograph taken for Mackintosh' Confectioners, showing the delicious contents of their Week End assortment.
The weekend was synonymous wit leisure and chocolates were considered a luxury. The image for Week End was one of leisure and luxury, of which chocolates were a integral part. A special gift for a special person. *C31643. 30/3/72.*

A press Ad for Edgar Allen Foundries, demonstrating that too large a proportion of the world's food production is lost.
8446. 25/8/64.

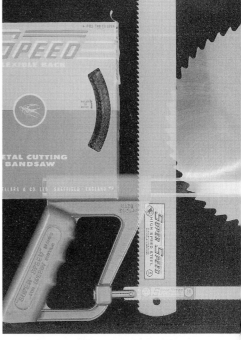

Another double exposure shot, showing a number of products on one photograph, with some parts transparent. This shot was taken for Slack Sellars & Co Ltd of Sheffield to promote their range of metal cutting blades. *8106. 11/5/64.*

This photograph shows many of the locally manufactured and distributed range of Hamax products. The shot was taken at Carlines in Mexborough.
10531/2. 21/9/66.

Mike's son Gareth poses for the camera in a photograph commissioned for Darwin's Magnets. The message seems to be that a Darwin magnet could pick up anything at all. *6876. 2/4/63.*

A pair of excellent pinking shears made in Sheffield and sold throughout the world. *7229. 17/9/63.*

Paul Walters at the beginning of his career as a photographic model? Paul is seen here with a professional model in a promotional shot for Trianco Boilers. *14327. 13/10/67.*

his photograph, taken at Doncaster racecourse, was to promote the 'Bramah' luxury
acuum flask. *10887. 13/12/66.*

n advertisment for the Edgar Allen tool company. Various measuring and drawing
nstruments are shown against an international background. The slide rule shown here
as since been replaced with the electronic calculator and computer. Anyone remember
ow to use one? *7270. 4/10/63.*

After trying various methods of launching the contents of a tin of Quality Street, the use of compressed air gave way to a bucket full of Mackintosh's finest confectionery being thrown up through a hole in the table. *C31645. 31/3/72.*

Taken for a Colbear Christmas advertising plan, this photograph was aptly titled 'Present Trouble'. *7328. 31/10/64.*

A press advertisement photograph shot for Earl Publishing Limited and entitle 'What's in it for me?' The shot was taken at Modern Foods in Mexboroug *10507. 13/9/65.*

WHITE ROSE PRESS.

The White Rose Press was the prestigious printing arm of the renowned South Yorkshire Times, until the late 1970's.

Like many newspapers, the South Yorkshire Times was opened under another name. The newspaper started life in 1877 when Walter Turner, a stationer in Mexborough, decided that the area really needed its' own newspaper and opened up the 'Mexborough and Swinton Times'. The paper flourished under this title until 1931, when the name was changed to the present 'South Yorkshire Times'.

During the 1880's, Walter Turner began using his press to do private work. This service continued and developed over the years until it became, in the fullness of time, the White Rose Press. Both the newspaper and the press businesses were run from the first offices of the newspaper on High Street, Mexborough. Despite considerable expansion of the premises over the years as business developed, it became obvious by 1962, that a new site had to be obtained.

In 1964, land situated between the canal and the railway station on Station Road, was purchased from the Town Council. This enabled premises of some 40,000 square feet of floor area to be constructed. From start to finish, the construction and equipping of the new plant took two years. The project cost in excess of £250,000 to complete, but the company was then equipped with high volume presses capable of very high quality work at very competitive prices.

The printing business flourished and a London office at a prestigious High Holborne address, sold the services of White Rose Press throughout London and the Home Counties. A marketing and sales department was also set up at the new Station Road premises and sold the services of White Rose Press throughout the north up to the Scottish border. Among the prestigious customer list were; the Royal Air Force, the Army, Firth Vickers Ltd, Swissair, J.C.B. Ltd, G.E.C. Ltd, and Power Gas.

Mike Walters had a close relationship with the company and was often called upon to produce the necessary photographic work for inclusion in catalogues, brochures etc.

The workforce at White Rose Press was considered to be particularly close knit and friendly, with a great pride in both the company and the work they produced.

The demise of the White Rose Press came in the late 1970's, when both the South Yorkshire Times and the allied White Rose Press where purchased by St Regis Press. St Regis owned a number of newspapers and had considerable existing print services to hand. The effect was a substantial reduction in the workload of White Rose Press, resulting in eventual closure. New offices were found in the town for the editorial staff and the printing plant and premises were sold.

Ken Geddes, (standing on left), in conference with the design team over the presentation of a corporate magazine. *18198/9. 12/7/68.*

Ian Boxhill, Compositor, demonstrates the art which today has, like so many other skills, fallen victim to computerisation. *18199/6. 12/7/68.*

An operator setting up the plates on the ro┐ Heidelberg press. These machines were at time capable of very high production rates once set up correctly. *18200/2. 12/7/68*

Barry Backhouse, standing with legs crossed, acts as head stone hand. Stan Doidge is also seen nearest the camera, demonstrating his skills to apprentice Keith Richardson as yet another production run is prepared. *18204/2. 12/7/68.*

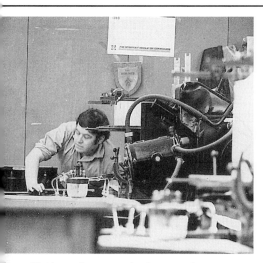

Gary Barker photographed operating
equipment at the Station Road plant. As a
founder of Mexborough Heritage, it is high
time Gary appeared in a publication
celebrating Mexborough's past. His father
appeared in our first publication, Industrial
South Yorkshire in Pictures, photographed
when he was employed at Denaby Powder
Works (ICI). *18202/3. 12/7/68.*

The Heidelberg presses, the heart of
White Rose Press, pour out a seemingly
endless stream of work. *18204/9. 12/7/68.*

Alice Tingle
collating pages prior
to sewing in the
binding room. As
can be seen from
the photograph, the
speed at which this
work was done was
quite phenomenal
and very accurate.
18202/4. 12/7/68.

Giles Brearley *(on the left)* is a Chartered Management Accountant in practice in Swinton. He was born at Barnsley, but resided at Mexborough. He went to college at High Melton, Doncaster, Sheffield and York. His father was Chief Public Health Inspector for Mexborough from 1940 until 1974. Giles has written other local history books – *Mexborough A Town At War* and *We Will Remember,* (jointly with Graham Oliver) and also wrote *History of Lead Mining in the Peak District* which was based on his years potholing in Derbyshire as a student.

ACKNOWLEDGEMENTS.

The authors would like to offer their thanks to those without whose assistance this book would not have been possible, among whom are:
Graham Oliver
John Stuart
Pat Walters
Roy Wooding
Diane Walters
Ian Boxhill
Walter Boxhill
Laird of Camster
for his South Yorkshire Notes

Paul Walters *(on the right)* began his professional career as a photographer in 1987. When he joined his father's company at the age of 24. His first task in learning the trade, was to assist Michael on a ten country tour of Europe for a multi-national company. It was this marathon 10,000 mile race around the continent that moulded the direction of Paul's career. Initially working with his father covering major building projects in addition to publications such as the APA guide to Athens, Michael managed to teach Paul not only the practical basics, but how to approach a subject to bring o its best characteristics. They worked together until he was forced into early retirement due to ill health. Michael wou use people to bring a subject to life and this is a technique Paul still uses in his work today.

Paul now spends much of his time overseas working for major travel companies, producing photographs for holiday brochures in addition to his UK based work in the production of pictures and exhibitions for Industry and Commerce